Love each other.

A Guide for Teaching

Ethics and Morals in Schools

Ethics Project

Acknowledgements

Ethics Project was born out of a vision to resurrect and enhance lost ethical and moral training in schools. The members of Ethics Project are educators from all facets of education: Para educators, superintendents, school board members, classroom teachers (active and retired), principals, professors, editors, and adjunct instructors.

Ethics Project Development Group

Desiree Mains, Teacher, Editor
Steve Urrutia, Teacher and Administrator
Julie Urrutia, Teacher
Steve McLain, Curriculum Administrator
Rick Cole, Professor and Superintendent
Kevin Gilman, Elementary Principal
Wendy Weld, Teacher
Win Taylor, School Board and Editor
Marcy Gonzalez, Para Educator
Jason Greene, Teacher
Jim Hopwood, Teacher
Mark Little, Teacher
Joy Bach, Editor
Dave Wiley, Project Advisor
Doug Radunzel, Project Advisor
Rich Korb, Educator, Writer, and Speaker
Karl Knudsen, Teacher and Administrator

Love each other.

Morals are the manifestation of ethics learned.

When the word love is spoken, it evokes many feelings and ideas. In actuality love is an emotion driven by attitudes. These attitudes are generated by life's experiences.

Love each other was created to challenge students and adults to evaluate love's impact on others. Within this booklet are sixteen stories coupled with lifestyle application activities. It is our hope that change in attitudes toward others will result in love demonstrated toward everyone.

How to implement the booklet? –

The booklet focuses on sixteen attributes of love. The booklet contains sixteen Love is . . . attribute stories from a variety of global resources bringing emphasis to each attribute of love.

1. Introducing one Love is . . . attribute story per month allows for concentrated practice of the attribute.
2. Each story is followed with elementary and secondary review questions about the story.
3. Each attribute concludes with an application challenge which teachers should discuss each day.
4. *Daily practice is essential for behavior change to occur.*
5. Each Love is . . . attribute has four reinforcement statements, one for each week of the month. The reinforcement statement is posted at the front of the room as a reminder to love each other.

Remember this

Daily practice is essential for behavior change to occur.

Ethics Project Team

Contents

Love is . . .

Attribute 15 - polite, respectful, courteous, thoughtful - 73

- o Attribute Stories:
  - ▪ *Consideration*
  - ▪ *We See Things Not The Way They Are, But The Way We Are.*
- o Attribute Activities
  - ▪ Story Discussion Prompts
  - ▪ Daily Lifestyle Application
- o Weekly Reinforcement Statements

Attribute 16 - kind, affectionate, gracious, understanding - 79

- o Attribute Story: *A 15-Year Blessing from A Homeless Person*
- o Attribute Activities
  - ▪ Story Discussion Prompts
  - ▪ Daily Lifestyle Application
- o Weekly Reinforcement Statements

"To educate a child in mind and not in morals is to educate a menace to society."

T. Roosevelt

16 Attributes of *Love*

Stories and Activities

Attribute 1

Love is persevering, determined, confident

Attribute Story

✓ **Story of the month group read**

Walt Disney – A True Story

As a young man, Walt Disney was fired from the *Kansas City Star* newspaper because his boss thought he lacked creativity. He went on to form an animation company called Laugh-O-Gram Films in 1921. Using his natural salesmanship abilities, Disney was able to raise $15,000 for the company ($197,474 in 2017 dollars). However, he made a deal with a New York distributor. When the distributor went out of business, Disney was forced to shut Laugh-O-Gram down. He could barely pay his rent and even resorted to eating dog food.

Broke but not defeated, Disney spent his last few dollars on a train ticket to Hollywood. Unfortunately, his troubles were not over. In 1926, Disney created a cartoon character named Oswald the Rabbit. When he attempted to negotiate a better deal with Universal Studios -- the cartoon's distributor -- Disney discovered Universal had secretly patented the Oswald character. Universal then hired Disney's artists away from him, and continued the cartoon without Disney's input and without paying him.

As if that weren't enough, Disney also struggled to release some of his now-classic films. He was told Mickey Mouse would fail because the mouse would "terrify women". Distributors rejected *The Three Little Pigs*, saying it needed more characters. *Pinocchio* was shut down during production, and Disney had to rewrite the entire storyline. Other films, like *Bambi*, *Pollyanna* and *Fantasia* were misunderstood by audiences at the time of their release, only to become favorites later on.

Disney's greatest example of perseverance occurred when he tried to make the book *Mary Poppins* into a film. In 1944, at the suggestion of his daughter, Disney decided to adapt the Pamela Travers novel into a screenplay. However, Travers had absolutely no interest in selling *Mary Poppins* to Hollywood. To win her over, Disney visited Travers at her England home repeatedly for the next 16 years. After more than a decade-and-a-half of persuasion, Travers was overcome by Disney's charm and vision for the film and finally gave him permission to bring *Mary Poppins* to the big screen. The result is a timeless classic.

In a fitting twist of fate, The Disney Company went on to purchase ABC in 1996. At the time, ABC was owner of the Kansas City Star. The newspaper that once fired Disney had become part of the empire he created thanks to his creativity and a lot of perseverance.

reference - http://www.growthink.com/content/7-entrepreneurs-whose-perseverance-will-inspire-you

Attribute Activities

Elementary

✓ **Story Discussion Prompts**

- How did Walt Disney show confidence in his artistic abilities?
- What do we enjoy from Walt Disney's determination and love for others?

✓ **Daily Life style Application**

- Demonstrate love for others by being determined to help them today.
- *Daily - Students and teacher share their experiences encouraging confidence in others.*

Secondary

✓ **Story Discussion Prompts**

- List the times Walt Disney demonstrated perseverance, determination, and confidence.

- What was Walt Disney's greatest example of love for others and what factor did perseverance play?

- What can we learn about love through Walt Disney's life?

✓ **Daily Lifestyle Application**

- Demonstrate love for others through acts of perseverance, determination and/or being confident today.

- *Daily - Students and teacher share their experiences demonstrating love for others through this month's attribute.*

Weekly Reinforcement Statements

(Post at the front of the classroom. Review daily.)

<u>Week 1</u> - Suffering produces perseverance; perseverance, character; and character, hope.

<u>Week 2</u> - A gossip betrays a confidence, but a trustworthy person keeps a secret.

<u>Week 3</u> - Do not disclose someone's confidence or you will be shamed and will never lose your bad reputation.

<u>Week 4</u> - Know that difficulties develop faith and perseverance.

Attribute 2 –

Love is encouraging, reassuring, supportive

Attribute Story

✓ **Story of the month group read**

Encouragement From a Mule

There was a farmer who owned an old mule. The mule fell into the farmer's well. The farmer heard the mule braying. After carefully assessing the situation, the farmer sympathized with the mule, but he decided that neither the mule nor the well was worth the trouble of saving. Instead, he called his neighbors together and enlisted them to help haul dirt to bury the old mule in the well and put him out of his misery.

Initially, the old mule was hysterical. But as the farmer and his neighbors continued shoveling and the dirt hit his back, a thought struck him. It suddenly dawned on him that every time a shovel load of dirt landed on his back, he would shake it off and step up. This he did, time after time.

"Shake it off and step up. Shake it off and step up," he repeated to encourage himself. No matter how painful the blows, or how distressing the situation seemed, the old mule fought panic and just kept right on shaking it off and stepping up.

It wasn't long before the mule, battered and exhausted, stepped triumphantly over the wall of that well. The dirt that seemed to bury him actually helped him, all because of the manner in which he handled his adversity.

This is like life. If we face our problems and respond to them positively, refusing to give in to panic, bitterness, or self-pity then the adversities that come along to bury us usually have within them the very real potential to benefit us.

reference - http://www.1stholistic.com/Reading/liv_the-farmer-and-the-mule-story.htm

Attribute Activities

Elementary

✓ **Story Discussion Prompts**

- What did the farmer ask his friends to do?

- What did the mule think about his situation?

- How did the mule solve his problem?

✓ **Daily Lifestyle Application**

- Demonstrate an act of encouragement for someone today.

- ***Daily*** *- Students and teacher share their experiences reassuring others.*

Secondary

✓ **Story Discussion Prompts**

- How did the mule react to being buried?

- What mental adjustment did the mule make to calm himself down?

- What action did the mule take to save his life?

- What can be the result of a positive outlook in times of trouble?

✓ **Daily Lifestyle Application**

- Demonstrate an act of encouragement, reassurance or support for someone today.

- *Daily - Students and teacher share their experiences demonstrating love for others through this month's attribute.*

Weekly Reinforcement Statements

(Post at the front of the classroom. Review daily.)

Week 1 - Practice fairness and encourage the discouraged.

Week 2 - Encourage each other and build each other up.

Week 3 - Grace gives us encouragement and hope.

Week 4 - Encouragement is shown through words and deeds.

Attribute 3 –

Love is considerate, modest, humane, tender, compassionate

Attribute Story

✓ **Story of the month group read**

Monday Musing: A Story about Being Considerate

Once upon a time, a man forgot to kiss his wife goodbye in the morning. This caused the wife to be grumpy. She went shopping and was rude to the sales clerk.

The sales clerk didn't like this treatment, so when another customer wanted help finding the exactly right sweater the clerk didn't have quite as much patience as she normally did.

The customer noticed and was offended. As the customer walked home, she picked up her teenage son from school. As they walked along, he started chattering about his day, but she wasn't really paying attention because she was thinking about the rude sales clerk.

The son, knowing that his mother wasn't paying attention, kicked a can into the path of an oncoming car just to see what would happen.

The driver swerved and swore loudly. He was still fuming about it when he reached his destination where he offloaded his disgust on to his friend over coffee.

The friend was slightly irritated by this. He had wanted to share his worries, but he had to listen to someone else's story instead. He got on the bus home and was rude to the bus driver.

reference - https://the57thsnowflake.wordpress.com

Attribute Activities

Elementary

✓ **Story Discussion Prompts**

- Why was the wife grumpy?

- How did her grumpiness affect others?

- What could someone have done to stop the grumpiness?

- ✓ **Daily Lifestyle Application**

  - Demonstrate stopping grumpiness today.

  - *Daily - Students and teacher share their experiences demonstrating compassion for others.*

Secondary

- ✓ **Story Discussion Prompts**

  - Why was the wife grumpy?

  - How many people were affected by the grumpy wife?

  - Discuss how each person was responsible for their actions.

- ✓ **Daily Lifestyle Application**

  - Demonstrate ways to control your reaction to others.

  - *Daily - Students and teacher share their experiences demonstrating love for others through this month's attribute.*

Weekly Reinforcement Statements

(Post at the front of the classroom. Review daily.)

<u>Week 1</u> - Slander no one and be considerate.

<u>Week 2</u> - Show true humility toward all people.

<u>Week 3</u> - Wisdom is pure, peace-loving, considerate, submissive, and full of mercy.

<u>Week 4</u> - Be kind and compassionate to each other, forgiving each other.

Attribute 4 –

Love is dependable, just, acceptable, equitable

Attribute Story

✓   **Story of the month group read**

Prince Lapio

There was once a very unfair Prince, although he seemed like the perfect Prince: handsome, brave, and intelligent. Prince Lapio gave the impression that no one had ever explained to him the nature of justice. If two people came to him over some dispute, expecting him to resolve the matter, he would decide in favor of whichever one seemed most charming, or most handsome, or whoever had the best-looking sword.

Tired of all this, Lapio's father, the King, decided to get a wise man to teach his son about justice. "My wise friend, please take him away," said the King, "and don't bring him back until he's ready to be a just and fair king."

The wise man left by boat with the Prince, but they suffered a shipwreck and ended up together, as the only survivors, on a desert island. There they had no food or water.

For the first few days, Prince Lapio, a great hunter, managed to catch some fish. When the wise old man asked him to share the fish with him, the young Prince refused. However, some days later, the Prince's fishing became less successful, while the old man was managing to catch birds almost every day. Just as the Prince had done, the wise man refused to share his catch. Lapio got thinner and thinner until he finally burst into tears and begged the wise man to share some of his food to save him from starving to death.

"I will only share them with you," said the wise man, "if you show me you've learned your lesson." The Prince, having learned what the wise man was trying to teach him, said, "Justice consists of sharing what we have equally."
The wise man congratulated him and gave him some food.

That same afternoon a ship rescued them from the island. On their return journey they stopped by a mountain, where a man recognized the Prince and told him: "I am Max, chief of the Maximum tribe. Please help us; we are having trouble with the neighboring tribe, the Minimums. We both share meat and vegetables yet we argue about how to share them."
"Very easily solved," answered the Prince, "Count how many of you there are altogether, and share the food in equal proportions." So he had already made good use of what the wise man had taught him.

But after saying this came the sound of thousands of cries from the mountainside. A hoard of angry men came running over, led by the chief who had asked the question. They leapt on Prince Lapio and took him prisoner.

Lapio couldn't understand this at all. They threw him in a prison cell and told him, "You tried to kill our people. If you don't solve this problem by daybreak tomorrow you will stay in prison forever."

They had done this to the Prince because the Minimums were small and numerous, whereas the Maximums were enormous, but there were very few of them. So the solution suggested by the Prince would have starved the Maximums to death. The Prince understood the situation and spent all that night thinking.

The next morning when they asked him for a solution the Prince said, "Don't share the food equally. Instead, share it according to how much each person eats. Give people food according to their size." The Maximums liked this answer so much that they released the Prince, held a great party, garlanded him with gold and jewels, and bid him and the wise man a safe journey.

As they were walking along the Prince commented, "I've learned something new. It is not fair to give the same to all. The fair thing is to share, but you must take people's differing needs into account." The wise man smiled with satisfaction.

Already close to the palace, they stopped in a small village. A man of very poor appearance received them and made sure they were well attended. Meanwhile, another man of similar poor appearance threw himself to the ground in front of them begging. A third, who seemed to be a rich man, sent two of his servants to tend to the Prince and the wise man providing them with what they needed. The Prince so enjoyed his time there that, on his departure, he presented the villagers with all the gold which the Maximums had given him. Hearing this, the poor man, the beggar, and the rich man all ran up to the Prince, each one asking for his share. "How will you share it?" asked the wise man, "The three are very different and it looks like the one who gives away more gold is the rich man."

The Prince hesitated. The wise man was right. The rich man had to pay his servants. He was the one who had spent the most gold, and he had looked after the servants well. However, the Prince was starting to develop a sense of justice and something told him that his first conclusion on this matter was not sufficient.

Finally, the Prince took his gold and made three piles: one very big, another medium sized, and the last one small. In that order he gave them to the poor man, the rich man, and the beggar. Saying his goodbyes, the Prince set off with the wise man heading back to the palace.

They walked in silence and when they reached the palace gate, the wise man asked, "Tell me something, young Prince. What does justice mean to you?"

"I think justice lies in sharing, taking into account necessities, but also the merits of the individual."

"Is that why you gave the smallest pile to the troublemaking beggar?" asked the wise man, contentedly.

"Yes, that's why. I gave the big pile to the poor man who looked after us so well. In him I saw both necessity and merit, since he helped us all he could, despite being poor. The medium pile was for the rich man. Even though he attended to us wonderfully, he really did not have much need for more gold. The small pile I gave to the bothersome beggar because he did nothing worthy of reward. However, given his great need, it was also right to give him something to live on," explained the Prince. "I think you'll be a fine King, Prince Lapio," concluded the wise man, embracing the Prince.

And he was right. From then on, the Prince became known throughout the kingdom for his fairness and wisdom. Some years later, his ascent to the throne was celebrated by all. And so it was that King Lapio became remembered as the best leader the kingdom had ever had.

Pedro Pablo Sacristán

Attribute Activities

Elementary

✓ **Story Discussion Prompts**

- Why did Prince Lapio get sent away from the kingdom?

- What did Prince Lapio do with the food he caught on the island?

- What did Prince Lapio learn from the wise man about sharing?

✓ **Daily Lifestyle Application**

- Demonstrate being fair and just today.

- ***Daily*** *- Students and teacher share their experiences being dependable for others.*

Secondary

✓ **Story Discussion Prompts**

- Why did Lapio's father send Lapio away?

- Describe Lapio's first lesson on justice and equity.

- What oversight did Lapio make about justice and equality between the Minimums and Maximums?

- What was Prince Lapio's final definition of justice?

✓ **Daily Lifestyle Application**

- Demonstrate justice while being dependable and accepting of others.

- Discuss - Where do we see justice in our world**?**

- *Daily* - *Students and teacher share their experiences demonstrating love for others through this month's attribute.*

Weekly Reinforcement Statements

(Post at the front of the classroom. Review daily.)

<u>Week 1</u> - Gain a disciplined life by doing what is right, just, and fair.

<u>Week 2</u> - The plans of the righteous are just, but the advice of the wicked is deceitful.

<u>Week 3</u> - The mouth of the righteous man utters wisdom and his tongue speaks what is just.

When justice is done, it brings joy to the righteous but terror to evildoers.

Attribute 5 –

Love is consistent, unfailing, eternal, inexhaustible, continual

Attribute Story

✓ **Story of the month group read**

A Story of Family And Unfailing Love

Once upon a time, a handsome young man asked a beautiful young woman to go out with him. She agreed, so he brought her to see Glenn Miller's dance band. It was his *first* first date. It was also his *last* first date. Not long after this date, they stood on her parents' porch, and he told her he loved her. He was going into the service, he said. Would she wait for him? She promised she would.

He was sent to England where he worked as a flight mechanic during the war. Sometimes he would send pilots out in the morning, and they would return unharmed in the afternoon. Sometimes he would send pilots out in the morning, and they would return with damaged planes in the afternoon. Sometimes he would send pilots out in the morning, and they would not return. Through it all, he and the woman stayed in touch through letters.

As soon as he stepped back onto American soil the man called her. "I'm home," he said. "How soon can we get married?" "How soon do you want to get married?" she asked in reply. Two weeks later they each said, "I do."

They settled down and started a family: two girls, a boy, then two more girls. They lived in the kind of neighborhood where kids played Kick the Can and grownups stopped to chat on the sidewalk. The kids fought in the way only siblings can, but they always remained best friends. The man and woman raised them to love God and each other.

The children grew and started families of their own. The man and woman became grandparents; first of one, then two, and eventually fifteen grandchildren. Despite the large number, each grandchild knew they held a unique place in their grandparents' hearts. Family gatherings were loud and filled with laughter. There were hard times, but always, there was love.

The older grandchildren began to marry, and the man and woman became great grandparents. The family decided to start numbering themselves in the order they joined the family. The total grew to over 40.

The woman got sick and battled cancer, the man always by her side. She fought bravely, but eventually the cancer won out. After 59 years of marriage, the man did the hardest thing he'd ever had to do, he said goodbye to the only woman he'd ever loved.

Eight more years passed in the blink of an eye. The man's body grew weaker, though his mind remained strong. One evening one of his granddaughters paid him a visit. They passed the hours reminiscing about this and that. She had always loved listening to his stories. Several times he gave his head a little shake and murmured, "Memories".

When it was time for bed, he said, "I say something like this each night: 'Now I lay me down to sleep. I pray the Lord my soul to keep. If I should die before I wake, I pray the Lord my soul to take.' Please be with my children. Please be with my grandchildren. That's about all I manage at night." He paused, and then he said, "I am blessed, *so* blessed." He looked lovingly at the picture of his wife beside his bed. "She sure knew how to raise children."

His granddaughter kissed his cheek and turned out the light. She went into the living room, spread a blanket on the couch, and smiled at the pillow with the embroidered saying, "Happiness is being married to your best friend."

As she lay down, she began to think about the man in the next room and the legacy he had created. He was still just as in love with his wife as that day long ago on her parents' porch. He could easily show hard hearted people the value of lifelong commitment. Every family that had formed as a result of the love of that man and woman was still happily intact.

As she drifted off to sleep, his words resonated in her head and in her heart, "I am blessed, *so* blessed."

reference - http://ohhonestly.net/the-legacy-a-story-of-family-and-unfailing-love/

Attribute Activities

Elementary

✓ **Story Discussion Prompts**

- What does this story teach us about love being continual?

- How did the husband demonstrate his love for his wife when she got sick?

- Do you think love can continue forever?

✓ **Daily Lifestyle Application**

- Demonstrate love toward someone today by saying, "Hi." Offering to hold a door open. Helping someone without being asked.

- *Daily - Students and teacher share their experiences being consistent with others.*

Secondary

✓ **Story Discussion Prompts**

- How did the couple demonstrate unfailing and inexhaustible love during the war?

- What tried to separate their love?

- How did their love prove to be continual?

- What impact did the love in their marriage have on their children and grandchildren?

✓ **Daily Lifestyle Application**

- Demonstrate unfailing love toward someone today.

- *Daily - Students and teacher share their experiences demonstrating love for others through this month's attribute.*

Weekly Reinforcement Statements

(Post at the front of the classroom. Review daily.)

<u>Week 1</u> - Constant practice of what is right trains one to know the difference between good and evil.

Week 2 - What people desire is unfailing love.

Week 3 - Many people claim to have unfailing love, but who can find a faithful person?

Week 4 - Sow for yourselves unfailing righteousness and reap the fruit of unfailing love.

Attribute 6 –

Love is protection, security, stability, shelter

Attribute Story

✓ **Story of the month group read**

Protection in Joplin – A True Story

The trees were glistening with silver.

Cheryl had never seen anything quite like it. The storm was coming, and she was going to outdrive it, or so she thought.

Cheryl had picked up her two daughters who were out celebrating a high school graduation in Joplin, Missouri. She thought she was driving away from the storm; but, her compass was backward, so she was actually driving square into it.

A half mile from home, rain started hammering down on 20th Street, the tornado's eventual destructive path on the night of May 22.

The rain was a deluge coming down so hard, as if she were in a car wash.

There could be no explanation for the magnitude of winds and rain bearing down. Cheryl realized she was in the midst of a massive tornado.

As the windows blew out, she pushed her daughters down and began to pray.

Suddenly, there was a peace that passed over them.

Cheryl and her two daughters were now in the vortex.

A split second later, the winds and rain picked up; and, in the blink of an eye, the van was whipped up into the twister, landing the van on the top of a roof that had been torn off a building.

They were smashed inside the van, covered by debris and wrapped in power lines.

A man came to their van with no debris on him. Cheryl felt a presence and peace. He said he was going to help them get out of the van. "You don't have to be afraid," he said as he helped them get out of the van.

As quickly as he appeared, he vanished.

reference - https://billygraham.org/story/a-story-of-gods-protection-in-joplin/#

Attribute Activities

Elementary

✓ **Story Discussion Prompts**

- Why did the mom and her daughters need protection?

- What act of love did the mom provide to protect her daughters?

- Who came to help the mom and her daughters?

✓ **Daily Lifestyle Application**

- Demonstrate love through protection or security for someone today.

- ***Daily*** - *Students and teacher share their experiences demonstrating protection for others.*

Secondary

✓ **Story Discussion Prompts**

- Why was the vortex a false sense of security?

- Describe two acts of love the mother demonstrated to protect her daughters.

- Based on the preceding story, explain – how love is protection, security, stability, and shelter.

✓ **Daily Lifestyle Application**

- Demonstrate love through providing stability for someone today, with security, protection.

- *Daily - Students and teacher share their experiences demonstrating love for others through this month's attribute.*

Weekly Reinforcement Statements

(Post at the front of the classroom. Review daily.)

Week 1 - May integrity and uprightness protect me.

Week 2 - Wise choices will protect you, and understanding will guard you.

Week 3 - Love guards the course of the just and protects the way of faithful ones.

Week <u>4</u> - Wisdom is a shelter and preserves the life of its

possessor.

Attribute 7 –

Love is righteous, virtuous, moral

Attribute Story

Note: Several stories are provided to allow for variety or best fit for the

age of the student.

✓ **Story of the month group read**

Honesty Is The Best Policy

A milkman became very wealthy through dishonest means. He had to

cross a river daily to reach the city where his customers lived. He

mixed the water of the river generously with the milk that he sold for

a good profit. One day he went around collecting the money due in

order to celebrate the wedding of his son. With the large amount thus collected, he purchased plenty of rich clothes and glittering gold ornaments. But while crossing the river, the boat capsized, and all his costly purchases were swallowed by the river. The milk vendor was speechless with grief. At that time he heard a voice that came from the river, "Do not weep. What you have lost is only the illicit gains you earned through cheating your customers."

Moral: Your dishonesty will find you out.

Night Watchman

The manager of a firm advertised for a night watchman.

Many of the applicants were present, but the manager was not satisfied.

He found something wrong with each one.

Raju was sitting in a corner waiting for his turn to be interviewed.

The manager found nothing wrong in his appearance.

He questioned him about his health.

Raju replied that he was suffering from sleeplessness.

Impressed with Raju's honesty, the manager was happy and appointed him.

Moral: Be honest.

One Nut and Two Boys

Two little boys were playing together. One little boy saw a nut on the ground. Before he could pick it up, the other boy took it.

The first boy demanded, "Give me the nut! It's mine! I saw it first!"

The other boy replied, "It's mine!"

This led to a quarrel between the two little boys. Just then an older boy came by. Upon seeing the quarrel between the boys, he said, "Give me the nut, and I'll settle your quarrel."

He split the nut into two parts. He took out the fruit-seed. He gave half of the shell to one boy and the other half to the other. He put the fruit seed into his mouth and said, "This is for settling your quarrel."

Moral: When two people quarrel no one wins.

The Wolf in Sheepskin

A wolf was walking in the countryside. He found a sheepskin spread on the ground. He thought, "If I wear this skin and get mixed up in the flock the shepherd will not suspect me. At night I will kill a stout sheep and then take the sheep away with me."

The wolf covered himself with the sheepskin and got mixed up with the flock of sheep. As he had expected, the shepherd thought he was a sheep and shut him in the pen. The wolf was waiting for night so he could steal one of the sheep.

The shepherd had a feast that night. He sent a servant to fetch a fat sheep. The servant selected the sheepskin covered wolf. That night, the guests had the wolf for supper.

Moral: Evil thoughts have evil ends.

reference - http://www.english-for-students.com

Attribute Activities

Elementary

✓ **Story Discussion Prompts**

- How do you think the story of the milkman would have ended if he was honest?

- Why did Raju get the job?

- What did arguing over the nut cost the two little boys?

- What did the wolf's disguise cost him?

✓ **Daily Lifestyle Application**

- Demonstrate honesty today.

- *Daily* - *Students and teacher share their experiences demonstrating love through honesty.*

Secondary

✓ **Story Discussion Prompts**

- Based on the river's comment to the crooked milkman, what did the milkman lose?

- How did Raju's honesty cause him to get the night watchman job?

- What could the two little boys have done to solve their problem so both were satisfied?

- What is the problem with presenting a false identity?

✓ **Daily Lifestyle Application**

- Demonstrate virtuous behaviors of righteousness today.

- **Daily** - *Students and teacher share their experiences demonstrating love for others through this month's attribute.*

Weekly Reinforcement Statements

(Post at the front of the classroom. Review daily.)

Week 1 - The wages of the righteous bring them life, but the income of the wicked brings them punishment.

Week 2 - The tongue of the righteous is choice silver, but the heart of the wicked is of little value.

Week 3 - Of all these virtues put on love, which binds them all together in perfect harmony.

Week 4 - The desire of the righteous ultimately ends in good, but the hope of the wicked ends in wrath.

Attribute 8 –

Love is thankful, grateful, satisfied, pleased

Attribute Story

✓ **Story of the month group read**

A Reference Point for Thankfulness

I know a man who has always been thankful for his shoes. When I asked him why, he replied, "When I was a boy during the Depression, my parents couldn't afford to buy new shoes for me. I put cardboard in my shoe bottoms whenever they got holes. When I walked through rain and snow, I had to keep replacing the cardboard. I've always been thankful for shoes because I've never forgotten wearing those shoes with holes in the soles."

His reference point for thankfulness was his childhood memory of worn-out shoes. If we will think of times when we did without, we'll become thankful for what we have.

reference - http://www.kentcrockett.com/cgi-bin/illustrations/index.cgi?topic=Thankfulness

Attribute Activities

Elementary

✓ **Story Discussion Prompts**

- What was the man thankful for?

- What caused the man to be thankful for his shoes?

- What can make us thankful?

✓ **Daily Lifestyle Application**

- Demonstrate thankfulness by thanking someone today.

- ***Daily*** - *Students and teacher share their experiences demonstrating thankfulness for others.*

Secondary

✓ **Story Discussion Prompts**

- What could the man's parents not afford to buy him during the Depression?

- How did the man make his shoes last longer?

- How did the man's childhood experience change his view about doing without?

✓ **Daily Lifestyle Application**

- Demonstrate thankfulness by thanking someone today.

- *Daily - Students and teacher share their experiences demonstrating love for others through this month's attribute.*

Weekly Reinforcement Statements

(Post at the front of the classroom. Review daily.)

Week 1 - Give thanks in all circumstances.

Week 2 - We should please others for their good, to build them up.

Week 3 - Try to please everybody in every way.

Week 4 - A fool finds pleasure in evil conduct.

Attribute 9 –

Love is promise keeping, hopeful, faithful, reliable

Attribute Story

✓ **Story of the month group read**

Don't Worry

A man had been on a long flight from one place to another. The first warning of the approaching problems came when the sign in the airplane flashed on: Fasten Your Seat Belts. Then, after a while, a calm voice said, "We will not be serving the beverages at this time as we are expecting a little turbulence. Please be sure your seat belt is fastened."

As he looked around the aircraft, it became obvious that many of the passengers were becoming apprehensive. Later, the voice of the pilot said, "We are so sorry that we are unable to serve the meal at this time. The turbulence is still ahead of us."

Then the storm broke. The ominous cracks of thunder could be heard even above the roar of the engines. Lightning lit up the darkening skies, and within moments that great plane was like a cork tossed around on a celestial ocean. One moment the airplane was lifted on terrific currents of air, then it dropped as if it were about to crash.

The man confessed he shared the discomfort and fear of those around him. He said, "As I looked around the plane, I could see that nearly all the passengers were upset and alarmed. Some were praying. The future seemed ominous and many were wondering if they would make it through the storm."

The man continued, "Then, I suddenly saw a little girl. Apparently the storm meant nothing to her. She had tucked her feet beneath her as she sat on her seat. She was reading a book, and everything within her small world was calm and orderly. Sometimes she closed her eyes, then she would read again, then she would straighten her legs, but worry and fear were not in her world. When the plane was being buffeted by the terrible storm, when it lurched this way and that as it rose and fell with frightening severity, when all the adults were scared half to death, that marvelous child was completely composed and unafraid." The man could hardly believe his eyes.

It was not surprising that when the plane finally reached its destination and all the passengers were hurrying to disembark, the man lingered to speak to the girl whom he had watched for such a long time. Having commented about the storm and behavior of the plane, he asked why she had not been afraid.

The child replied, "Cause my Daddy's the pilot, and he's taking me home."

reference - http://www.inspire21.com/stories/faithstories/dontworry

Attribute Activities

Elementary

✓ **Story Discussion Prompts**

- Why did the little girl trust her father?

- Why do you think the passengers were praying?

- How could having love for someone give hope to others?

✓ **Daily Lifestyle Application**

- Demonstrate love by keeping a promise today.

- *Daily - Students and teacher share their experiences keeping a promise with others.*

Secondary

✓ **Story Discussion Prompts**

- What does faith have to do with love?

- Why do you think other passengers prayed about their situation?

- What can we learn about love and trust through the pilot's daughter?

✓ **Daily Lifestyle Application**

- Demonstrate love for others through being hopeful, faithful, keeping promises, or being reliable today.

- *Daily - Students and teacher share their experiences demonstrating love for others through this month's attribute.*

Weekly Reinforcement Statements

(Post at the front of the classroom. Review daily.)

<u>Week 1</u> - Suffering produces perseverance, perseverance character and character hope.

<u>Week 2</u> - Be joyful in hope and patient in times of trouble.

<u>Week 3</u> - Concentrating on problems is the focus of the unfaithful in times of trouble.

<u>Week 4</u> - Let love and faithfulness never leave you.

Attribute 10 –

Love is pleasant, peacekeeping, cheerful, calm

Attribute Story

✓   **Story of the month group read**

The Peacemaker

Carl and Sam were upset with each other. They could not even remember the initial cause of the anger, but their hostility had festered through the years. A deeply concerned friend prayed that God would use him as a peacemaker.

The peacemaker went to Carl and asked, "What do you think of Sam?"

"He's the sorriest guy in town!" Carl replied.

"But," countered the peacemaker, "you have to admit that he's a hard-working man."

"No one can deny that." said Carl.

"I've never known a person who worked harder."

Next, the peacemaker visited Sam. "Do you know what Carl said about you?" "No, but I can imagine his lies." Sam responded angrily.

"This may surprise you," said the peacemaker, "but he said he's never known a harder worker."

"He said that?" Sam was stunned.

"What do you think of Carl?" asked the peacemaker.

"It is no secret that I have absolutely no use for him." Sam replied.

"But you must admit he's honest in business." said the peacemaker.

"There's no getting around that." said Sam. "In business he's a man you can trust."

Later, the peacemaker met Carl again. "Do you know what Sam said about you? He claims you're absolutely trustworthy in business, that you are scrupulously honest." "Well, how 'bout that." smiled Carl.

Soon the peacemaker noticed Sam and Carl would cautiously nod in a friendly sort of way. Before long they were shaking hands, talking, even visiting in each others' homes.

Today they are best friends.

reference - http://www.spiritual-short-stories.com/spiritual-short-story-519-How+Can+You+Be+a+Peacemaker++.html

Attribute Activities

Elementary

✓ **Story Discussion Prompts**

- Why were Carl and Sam upset with each other?

- Why do you think the friend/peacemaker wanted to help his friends?

- What happened to Carl and Sam after their friend helped them?

✓ **Daily Lifestyle Application**

- Demonstrate a pleasant and cheerful attitude toward someone today.

- *Daily - Students and teacher share their experiences demonstrating a cheerful attitude for others.*

Secondary

✓ **Story Discussion Prompts**

- Why were Carl and Sam upset with each other, and for how long had they been upset?

- Why is it beneficial to help friends see the good in others?

- How could Carl and Sam's anger effect other relations they had?

- How did Sam and Carl begin the healing process?

✓ **Daily Lifestyle Application**

- Demonstrate peacekeeping by being cheerful, pleasant, and staying calm today.

- *Daily - Students and teacher share their experiences demonstrating love for others through this month's attribute.*

Weekly Reinforcement Statements

(Post at the front of the classroom. Review daily.)

Week 1 - Turn from evil and do good; seek peace and pursue it.

Week 2 - A cheerful look brings joy to the heart and good news gives health to the body.

Week 3 - A hot temper stirs up trouble, but a patient person calms an argument.

Week 4 - Pleasant words are as honey, sweet to the soul and

healing to the body.

Attribute 11 –

Love is trusting, believing, confiding

Attribute Story

✓ **Story of the month group read**

The Miracle of $1.11

Tess was a precocious eight year old when she heard her mom and dad talking about her little brother, Andrew. All she knew was that he was very sick, and they were completely out of money. They were moving to an apartment complex next month because her father didn't have the money for the doctor bills and the house. Only a very costly surgery could save her brother now, and it was looking like there was no one to loan them money. She heard her father say to her tearful mother with whispered desperation, "Only a miracle can save him now."

Tess went to her bedroom and pulled a glass jar from its hiding place in the closet. She poured all the change out on the floor and counted it carefully three times. The total had to be exactly perfect. Carefully placing the coins back in the jar and twisting on the cap, she slipped out the back door and made her way six blocks to a drugstore with her money. She waited patiently for the pharmacist to give her some attention, but he was too busy at this moment. Tess twisted her feet to make a scuffing noise, no reaction. She cleared her throat with the most disgusting sound she could muster, still no response.

Finally, she took a quarter from her jar and banged it on the glass counter. That did it!

"And what do you want?" the pharmacist asked in an annoyed tone of voice. "I'm talking to my brother from Chicago whom I haven't seen in ages," he said without waiting for a reply to his question.

"Well, I want to talk to you about my brother," Tess answered back in the same annoyed tone. "He's really; really sick and I want to buy a miracle."

"I beg your pardon?" said the pharmacist.

"His name is Andrew and he has something bad growing inside his head, and my daddy says only a miracle can save him now. So how much does a miracle cost?"

"We don't sell miracles here, little girl. I'm sorry, but I can't help you," the pharmacist said, softening a little. "Listen", the little girl said, "I have the money to pay for it. If it isn't enough, I will get the rest. Just tell me how much it costs."

The pharmacist's brother was a well dressed man. He stooped down and asked the little girl, "What kind of a miracle does your brother need?"

"I don't know," Tess replied with her eyes welling up. "I just know he's really sick, and Mommy says he needs an operation. But my daddy can't pay for it, so I want to use my money."

"How much do you have?" asked the man from Chicago. "One dollar and eleven cents is all I have," Tess answered barely audibly. "And it's all the money I have, but I can get some more if I need to."

"Well, what a coincidence," smiled the man. "A dollar and eleven cents – the exact price of a miracle for little brothers." He took her money in one hand and with the other hand he grasped her mitten and said, "Take me to where you live. I want to see your brother and meet your parents. Let's see if I have the kind of miracle you need."

That well-dressed man was Dr. Carlton Armstrong, a surgeon specializing in neurosurgery. The operation was completed without charge, and it wasn't long until Andrew was home again and doing well. Mom and Dad were happily talking about the chain of events that had led them to this place.

"That surgery," her mother whispered, "was a real miracle. I wonder how much it would have cost."

Tess smiled. She knew exactly how much a miracle cost -- one dollar and eleven cents -- plus the faith of a little child.

reference-http://academictips.org/blogs/the-miracle-of-1-11-true-story/

Attribute Activities

Elementary

✓ **Story Discussion Prompts**

- How did Tess's act of love help her brother?

- How did believing in a miracle change Tess's parents?

- Which adult brother showed the most love and why?

✓ **Daily Lifestyle Application**

- Demonstrate love by trusting someone today.

- ***Daily*** *- Students and teacher share their experiences demonstrating trust for others.*

Secondary

✓ **Story Discussion Prompts**

- How did Tess's love for her brother affect the pharmacist and his brother?

- How did Tess's actions cause the doctor to help her brother?

- How did the doctor's love impact Tess's family?

✓ **Daily Lifestyle Application**

- Demonstrate love by confiding in someone's integrity today.

- ***Daily*** *- Students and teacher share their experiences demonstrating love for others through this month's attribute.*

Weekly Reinforcement Statements

(Post at the front of the classroom. Review daily.)

Week 1 - Stop trusting in what is worthless or you will get nothing in return.

Week 2 - A simple man believes anything, but a wise man gives thought to his steps.

Week 3 - God confides in those who fear him.

Week 4 - Do not throw away your confidence. It will be richly rewarded.

Attribute 12 –

Love is truthful, believable, reliable, sincere

Attribute Story

✓ **Story of the month group read**

The Story of Truth And A Story about Truth

Truth walked into a village. The local inhabitants started cursing at him. Spewing epithets, they chased him out of the village.

Truth walked along the road to the next town. They spat at him, cursed and spewed epithets, driving him out of town.

He walked lonely and sad down the empty road until he reached the next town, still hoping to find someone who was happy to see him, who would embrace Truth with open arms.

So he walked into the third town, this time in the middle of the night, hoping that dawn would find the townsfolk happy to see Truth with dawn's light. As soon as the townsfolk saw him, they ran to their homes and then came back throwing garbage at him.

Truth ran off, out of town, into the woods. After crying and cleaning off the garbage, he returned to the edge of the woods. There he heard laughter and gaiety, singing and applause. He saw the townsfolk applauding as Story entered the town. They brought out fresh meats and soups and pies and pastries and offered them all to Story, who smiled and lavished in their love and appreciation.

Come twilight, Truth was sulking and sobbing at the edge of the woods. The townsfolk disdainfully ignored him, but Story came out to see what the issue was.

Truth told Story how all the townsfolk mistreated him, how sad and lonely he was, and how much he wanted to be accepted and appreciated.

Story replied, "Of course they all reject you." Story looked at Truth, eyes a bit lowered to the side. "No one wants to look at the truth."

So Story gave Truth brilliant, beautiful clothing to wear. They walked into the town together, Truth with Story. The townspeople greeted them with warmth, love and appreciation, for Truth, wrapped in Story's clothing, was a beautiful thing and easy to behold.

Ever since then Truth travels with Story, and they are always accepted and loved. And that's the way it was, and the way it is, and the way it will always be.

reference - http://www.henshall.com/blog/archives/000156.html

Attribute Activities

Elementary

✓ **Story Discussion Prompts**

- Why is it hard to tell the truth?

- Why do you think the townspeople like Story more than Truth?

- How is telling the truth an act of love?

- How could you tell the truth with a story?

✓ **Daily Lifestyle Application**

- Demonstrate love by being truthful today.

- *Daily* - *Students and teacher share their experiences demonstrating truthfulness with others.*

Secondary

✓ **Story Discussion Prompts**

• Why did the townspeople demonstrate love to Story over Truth?

• How did Truth dressing like Story gain the love of the townspeople?

• Why is it hard to tell the truth in love?

✓ **Daily Lifestyle Application**

• Demonstrate love by being truthful, believable, reliable, and sincere today.

• *Daily* - *Students and teacher share their experiences demonstrating love for others through this month's attribute.*

Weekly Reinforcement Statements

(Post at the front of the classroom. Review daily.)

Week 1 - I have chosen the way of truth.

Week 2 -   People take pleasure in honest lips; they value a person who speaks the truth.

Week 3 -   A simple person believes anything, but a wise person thinks about his path.

Week 4 -   Love must be sincere. Hate what is evil; cling to what is good.

Attribute 13 –

Love is humble, meek, modest, quiet

Attribute Story

✓ **Story of the month group read**

To Humble Ourselves – A True Story

I was parked in front of the mall wiping off my car. I had just come from the car wash and was waiting for my husband to get out of work.

Coming my way from across the parking lot was what society would consider a homeless person. From the looks of him, he had no car, no home, no clean clothes, and no money. There are times when I feel generous, but there are other times that I just don't want to be bothered. This was one of those I don't want to be bothered times.

I hope he doesn't ask me for any money, I thought. He didn't. He came and sat on the curb in front of the bus stop, but he didn't look like he could have enough money to even ride the bus.

After a few minutes he spoke, "That's a very pretty car." he said.

I said, "Thanks," and continued wiping off my car. He sat there quietly as I worked. The expected plea for money never came.

As the silence between us widened, something inside said, "Ask him if he needs any help." I was sure he would say "yes", but I held true to the inner voice.

"Do you need any help?" I asked.

He answered in three simple, but profound words I shall never forget. I expected nothing but an outstretched grimy hand. He spoke the three words that shook me.

"Don't we all?" he said.

I was feeling high and mighty, successful and important, above a bum in the street, until those three words hit me like a twelve gauge shotgun.

"Don't we all?"

I needed help. Maybe not for bus fare or a place to sleep, but I needed help. I reached in my wallet and gave him not only enough for bus fare, but enough to get a warm meal and shelter for the day.

We often look for wisdom in great men and women. We expect it from those of higher learning and accomplishments.

No matter how much you have or how much you have accomplished, you need help too.

No matter how little you have or how loaded you are with problems, even without money or a place to sleep, you can give help.

Even if it's just a compliment, you can give that.

Maybe the man was just a homeless stranger wandering the streets.

Maybe he was more than that . . . .

reference - http://www.citehr.com/116663-true-touching-story-humble-ourselves.html

Attribute Activities

Elementary

✓ **Story Discussion Prompts**

- What is a homeless person?

- Why do people stay away from homeless persons?

- Why did the lady ignore the homeless person?

- What did the lady do for the homeless person?

- What did the homeless person say to the lady when she asked him, "Do you need any help?"

✓ **Daily Lifestyle Application**

- Demonstrate putting someone first today.

- *Daily - Students and teacher share their experiences demonstrating others first.*

Secondary

✓ **Story Discussion Prompts**

- Why did the lady avoid the homeless person?

- What did the lady think he was going to ask her?

- What words would the lady never forget and why?

- Why did the lady believe we all need help?

- What ways did the lady suggest we could do to help someone?

- What was the lady suggesting about who the homeless stranger might have been?

✓ **Daily Lifestyle Application**

- Demonstrate humility today.

- *Daily - Students and teacher share their experiences demonstrating love for others through this month's attribute.*

Weekly Reinforcement Statements

(Post at the front of the classroom. Review daily.)

<u>Week 1</u> - Grace is the reward for the humble.

<u>Week 2</u> - Humble yourself, and you will be honored.

<u>Week 3</u> - Whoever is proud will be humbled.

<u>Week 4</u> - Humility teaches wisdom.

Attribute 14 –

Love is patient, tolerant, calm, gentle

Attribute Story

✓ **Story of the month group read**

The Taxi Driver

I arrived at the address and honked the horn. After waiting a few

minutes I honked again. Since this was going to be the last ride of my

shift, I thought about just driving away, but instead I put the car in

park and walked up to the door and knocked. "Just a minute," answered a frail, elderly voice. I could hear something being dragged across the floor.

After a long pause, the door opened. A small woman in her 90's stood before me. She was wearing a print dress and a pillbox hat with a veil pinned on it, like somebody out of a 1940's movie. By her side was a small nylon suitcase. The apartment looked as if no one had lived in it for years. All the furniture was covered with sheets. There were no clocks on the walls, no knickknacks or utensils on the counters. In the corner was a cardboard box filled with photos and glassware.

"Would you carry my bag out to the car?" she said. I took the suitcase to the cab, then returned to assist the woman. She took my arm, and we walked slowly toward the curb. She kept thanking me for my kindness. "It's nothing," I told her. "I just try to treat my passengers the way I would want my mother to be treated." "Oh, you're such a good boy," she said.

When we got in the cab, she gave me an address and then asked, "Could you drive through downtown?" "It's not the shortest way," I answered quickly. "Oh, I don't mind," she said. "I'm in no hurry. I'm on my way to hospice."

I looked in the rear-view mirror. Her eyes were glistening. "I don't have any family left," she continued in a soft voice. "The doctor says I don't have very long." I quietly reached over and shut off the meter. "What route would you like me to take?" I asked.

For the next two hours, we drove through the city. She showed me the building where she had once worked as an elevator operator. We drove through the neighborhood where she and her husband had lived when they were newlyweds. She had me pull up in front of a furniture warehouse that had once been a ballroom where she had gone dancing as a girl. Sometimes she'd ask me to slow in front of a particular building or corner and would sit staring into the darkness, saying nothing. As the first hint of sun was creasing the horizon, she suddenly said, "I'm tired. Let's go now."

We drove in silence to the address she had given me. It was a low building, like a small convalescent home with a driveway that passed under a portico. Two orderlies came out to the cab as soon as we pulled up. They were solicitous and intent, watching her every move. They must have been expecting her. I opened the trunk and took the small suitcase to the door. The woman was already seated in a wheelchair. "How much do I owe you?" she asked, reaching into her purse. "Nothing." I said. "You have to make a living," she answered. "There will be other passengers" I responded. Almost without thinking, I bent and gave her a hug. She held onto me tightly. "You gave an old woman a little moment of joy," she said. "Thank you," I said and squeezed her hand, then walked into the dim morning light. Behind me, a door shut. It was the sound of the closing of a life.

I didn't pick up any more passengers that shift. I drove aimlessly lost in thought. For the rest of that day I could hardly talk. What if that woman had an angry driver, or one who was impatient to end his shift? What if I had refused to take the run, or had honked once, then driven away?

On a quick review, I don't think that I have done anything more important in my life. We're conditioned to think that our lives revolve around great moments. But great moments often catch us unaware beautifully wrapped in what others may consider a small one.

reference - http://elitedaily.com/life/culture/story-one-taxi-driver-will-change-entire-day/

Attribute Activities

Elementary

✓ **Story Discussion Prompts**

- Why did the old lady say, "You're such a good boy"?

- Why do you think the taxi driver agreed to drive the old lady around town?

- Why do you think the taxi driver refused to take the old lady's money?

- Why do you think the taxi driver gave the old lady a hug?

✓ **Daily Lifestyle Application**

- Demonstrate patience of understanding to someone today.

- *Daily* - *Students and teacher share their experiences demonstrating patience for others.*

Secondary

✓ **Story Discussion Prompts**

- What did the taxi driver say that made the old lady respond with, "You're such a good boy"?

- What do you think caused the taxi driver to turn off the fare meter?

- Why do you think the taxi driver was willing to drive the old lady around town for free?

- Why do you think the taxi driver thought, ". . . I don't think that I have done anything more important in my life"?

✓ **Daily Lifestyle Application**

- Demonstrate patience and tolerance in a gentle way today.

- *Daily - Students and teacher share their experiences demonstrating love for others through this month's attribute.*

Weekly Reinforcement Statements

(Post at the front of the classroom. Review daily.)

Week 1 - A patient person has understanding, but a quick-tempered person is foolish.

Week 2 - If you are righteous, you cannot tolerate wrong.

Week 3 - Be humble, gentle and patient treating each other in love.

Week 4 - Let your gentleness be seen by all.

Attribute 15 –

Love is polite, respectful, courteous, thoughtful

Attribute Stories

Note: Several stories are provided to allow for variety or best fit for the age of the students.

✓ **Story of the month group read**

Story 1

Consideration

One day a ten year old boy went to an ice cream shop sat at a table and asked the waitress, "How much is an ice cream cone?" She said, "Seventy-five cents." The boy started counting the coins he had in his hand. Then he asked how much a small cup of ice cream was. The waitress impatiently replied, "Sixty-five cents." The boy said, "I will have the small ice cream cup." He ate his ice cream, paid the bill, and left. When the waitress came to pick up the empty cup, she was touched. Underneath the cup was ten cents as a tip.

The little boy had consideration for the waitress before he ordered his ice cream. He showed sensitivity and caring. He thought of others before himself.

If we all thought like the little boy, we would have a great place to live. Show consideration, courtesy, and politeness.

Thoughtfulness shows a caring attitude.

Story 2

We See Things Not The Way They Are, But The Way We Are.

There is a legend about a wise man who was sitting outside his village. A traveler came up and asked him, "What kind of people live in this village, because I am looking to move from my present one?" The wise man asked, "What kinds of people live where you want to move from?" The man said, "They are mean, cruel, and rude." The wise man replied, "The same kind of people live in this village too." After some time another traveler came by and asked the same question and the wise man asked him, "What kind of people live where you want to move from?" The traveler replied, "The people are very kind, courteous, polite and good." The wise man said, "You will find the same kind of people here too."

What is the moral of the story?

Generally, we see the world not the way it is but the way we are. Most of the time, other people's behavior is a reaction to our own.

reference - http://great-motivational-stories.blogspot.com

Attribute Activities

Elementary

✓ **Story Discussion Prompts Story 1**

- Why did the little boy ask about the price of ice cream?

- What did the little boy do to show he cared about the waitress?

- How much did he leave for the waitress?

- How old was the boy?

✓ **Daily Lifestyle Application**

- Demonstrate an act of politeness to someone today.

- *Daily* - *Students and teacher share their experiences demonstrating politeness for others.*

✓ **Story Discussion Prompts Story 2**

- Who sat outside the village?

- Who stopped to talk with the wise man?

- What did the travelers want?

- What kind of people lived in the village?

✓ **Daily Lifestyle Application**

- Demonstrate respect to someone today.

Secondary

✓ **Story Discussion Prompts Story 1**

- What provisions did the little boy make before he bought ice cream?

- Who did the little boy consider first before he bought ice cream?

- How did the little boy show favor toward the impatient waitress?

- How did the waitress's attitude affect the little boy's tip?

✓ **Daily Lifestyle Application**

- Demonstrate acts of politeness, respect, courtesy, and thoughtfulness toward others today.

✓ **Story Discussion Prompts Story 2**

- Why do you think the wise man sat outside the village?

- How was the response to both travelers similar yet different?

- How is it possible that in one village an attitude of cruelty and meanness are predominate, yet in the other village there appears to be sentiments of kindness, courtesy, politeness and good?

- What is the moral of the story?

✓ **Daily Lifestyle Application**

- Demonstrate acts of politeness, respect, courtesy, and thoughtfulness toward others today.

- *Daily - Students and teacher share their experiences demonstrating love for others through this month's attribute.*

Weekly Reinforcement Statements

(Post at the front of the classroom. Review daily.)

Week 1 - Those who respect instruction will be rewarded.

Week 2 - Show respect to everyone.

Week 3 - A kind hearted person gains respect.

Week 4 - Rise in the presence of the elderly.

Attribute 16 –

Love is kind, affectionate, gracious, understanding

Attribute Story

✓ **Story of the month group read**

A 15-Year Blessing from A Homeless Person

On the way back from work every evening, more often than not, there would be a homeless man standing at the exit of the freeway. He looked to be in his late 40's, but was probably a lot younger. He had shoulder-length straight black hair, a short beard, and he was of average stature.

His eyes were what struck me the most about him. They were brown and had a sparkle, like an inside light that was beaming out. People say they can tell a lot from a person's eyes. It was certainly true in his case. He always waved at every car. He was always happy and smiling and sometimes almost dancing.

Every day after work I would remember to gather any spare change and put it aside to give to him if I saw him. A feeling of joy would come over me every time I saw him as I came off the ramp. He had that effect.

I'd quickly roll down my window and give him the coins. Occasionally, the red light would be on for a minute and we would ask each other about our day. His answer would always be the same, "I'm blessed!"

I knew what his answer was going to be every time, yet I would still ask. It amazed me that even in his situation of being homeless he was so positive. His answer would remind me of how blessed I was to be a single mother of four amazing kids, with a place to call home and a job to provide for my kids.

Then one day I was called into my boss's office and was told I was being laid off due to the economy. A feeling of worry engulfed me, and for the rest of that day all I could think of was, "How am I going to provide for my kids, how am I going to pay rent, what am I going to do?"

Needless to say, on my way home I was very sad and upset. I didn't remember to look for my spare change like I usually did. I wasn't feeling joy as I got off the ramp where the homeless man would be. Yet there he was, as always, as I turned down the ramp. He set his eyes on me, while still smiling and waving at others.

I'd hoped to catch the green light, but I missed it. While I was waiting for the red light to turn, he strolled over to my car. He had a big smile, he looked me straight in the eyes and said, "Today I will give you a dollar." He then reached into his pocket and pulled out a dollar bill. I was blown away. I burst into tears. I wanted to jump out of my car and hug him!

You see he gave me more than a dollar bill. He taught me a valuable lesson. No matter what material things are taken from you, no one can take away your choice to be joyful. My ride home was smooth sailing. I had lost my job and had no savings, but I knew I was blessed!

Every time I'm faced with challenges, I think of the homeless man's valuable lesson and remember that I am blessed.

reference - http://www.kindspring.org

Attribute Activities

Elementary

✓ **Story Discussion Prompts**

- What did the lady like about the homeless man?

- How did the lady help the homeless man?

- How did the homeless man help the lady?

- What did the lady learn from her talks with the homeless man?

✓ **Daily Lifestyle Application**

- Demonstrate being kind to someone today.

- *Daily* - *Students and teacher share their experiences demonstrating kindness toward others.*

Secondary

✓ **Story Discussion Prompts**

- What was it about the homeless man's eyes that encouraged the lady to help him?

- What do you think caused the lady to give money and talk with the homeless man?

- List three things the homeless man did for the lady that gave her hope.

- What was the significance of the homeless man giving a dollar to the lady?

✓ **Daily Lifestyle Application**

- Demonstrate kindness, grace, and understanding toward someone today.

- *Daily - Students and teacher share their experiences demonstrating love for others through this month's attribute.*

Weekly Reinforcement Statements

(Post at the front of the classroom. Review daily.)

Week 1 - A kind person improves himself, but a cruel person brings trouble to himself.

Week 2 - Honored is the individual who finds wisdom and understanding.

Week 3 - He who is kind to the poor will be rewarded for what he has done.

Week 4 - A fool finds pleasure in evil conduct, but a person of understanding delights in wisdom.

Made in the USA
Coppell, TX
20 November 2019

11651607R00052